The North End

by

Judith Robbins

The North End

Copyright © 2016 by Judith Robbins

All rights reserved. No part of this book may be reproduced or transmitted in any form or by any means without written permission of the author.

ISBN 978-1-943424-10-8

Library of Congress Control Number: 2016939744

North Country Press
Unity, Maine

To Jon …

Acknowledgments

Christianity and Literature My Retinue

The Blue Collar Review CONDEMNED
The Day after Payday
Downstairs Neighbor
Dependence

Puckerbrush Review Saturday Sauna
Reclaiming
After Seamus Heaney's "Seeing Things III"
In morte vita

Iltatahti On Hearing Finnish Spoken after Many Years

Potato Eyes My Mother Hanging Clothes in January

The Other Side The Men at Lincoln Square

Feminist Times Ironing and Smoking
Conjuring

Echoes Spelling Czechoslovakia
Q. Why Don't You Move South for the Winter?
Metaphysician in Overshoes

St. Anthony Messenger   Mourning Anew

The Worcester Review   Poets Hill
                                The Ides of March
                                First Cigarette

The American Scholar   Fragment

Phoebe   Cutting My Daughter's Hair
                                    Down by the Pasture

Belfast Republican Journal   Porpentine

Table of Contents

My Retinue / 1
Repentance / 2
"Mixed Marriage" / 3
CONDEMNED / 5
Ditching / 7
Kapishes' Back Yard / 8
The Men at Lincoln Square / 9
Tony's Candy Store / 10
Bobby / 11
Katy / 12
I'll Show You, Freddie / 13
Albie / 14
Jackie / 15
Icon / 17
Mrs. Jaatinen / 19
Dependence / 21
Downstairs Neighbor / 22
On Hearing Finnish Spoken after Many Years / 23
Saturday Sauna / 24
Conjuring My Mother / 25
Reclaiming / 26
My Mother Hanging Clothes in January / 27
Bringing Up the Oil / 28
Runaways / 29
Ironing and Smoking / 30
The Morning after Payday / 31
Spelling Czechoslovakia / 32
Sacred Ground / 33
Miss Cronin's Room / 34
Jounces / 35
The Friday Night Fights / 36

After Seamus Heaney's "Seeing Things III" / 37
Aiden Kieli / 38
Mourning Anew / 39
Poets Hill / 40
Q. Why Don't You Move South for the Winter? / 42
Porpentine / 43
Metaphysician in Overshoes / 44
March to Spring / 45
Secular Sainthood / 46
The Ides of March / 47
Fragment / 48
Listen, Look / 51
Graduation Day, Eastport, Maine / 52
First Cigarette / 53
Cutting My Daughter's Hair Down by the Pasture / 55
Watching for the Haymaker / 56
I forgot to tell you… / 57
Cheers! / 58
Day of Darkness / 59
Be-fogged in Maine: A Visitation / 60
For Philip Booth, Still / 61
Rhubarb Lust / 62
Early on a Late August Morning / 64
When first I lit the October stove / 65
Open Season / 66
In morte vita / 67
Relationship / 68
Trying to Take Responsibility / 69
Train in Gardiner / 70

Drawing of her house, by the author, age 5.

My Retinue

Raise up the story of your grave past
from beneath the stone foundation
of your first house

where blocked in living cement
you lived like an anchoress
attached to a church

closed in and fed
by an unseen hand
through an opening in the wall.

You survived the enclosure
until the iconoclast of your own desire
dismantled that wall

stone by stone
and you stepped forth
finding yourself full grown.

From stones of stories set aside
build a foundation for another house,
where I will come and keep you, my retinue.

Repentance

I can't remember your name—
something odd for a child, like Victor or Virgil—
A quiet child, you came as clear
>	as a photograph,
>	a neighborhood map
>	imprinted on your pale face
>	an invitation to return with you
>	to the North End, where I grew up
>	tormenting you, as children themselves
>	tormented do, the pecking order of hens
>		in an urban setting.

Shamer of conscience, you opened the pages
of a history shut these many years.
So does the pilgrim pick up her pack
to walk the road back with you
into a past that demands its pound of flesh.

"Mixed Marriage"
for my mother

The first time she saw the house
she tried to hide dismay—
shingles fallen from the roof
a bow in the sill that boded ill
for a sure foundation to withstand
the winter storms. Her husband's
ebullience at providing shelter
in his signature city
overcame her practical fears
for the time being, young and carrying
their first child, together they climbed
the stairs to the four rooms that would be home
for the length of their mixed marriage.

How did she feel signing us over
unborn as we were when they were married?

Do you promise to raise children born of this union Catholic?

She did and faithfully fulfilled that promise
in a culture whose language was not her own
whose rituals tripped her up
       from the very beginning
like the peasant girl of fairy tale out of place
in the king's castle, she made her deal
       with Rumpelstiltskin
providing the king with legitimate heir and working
with the straw that she was given.
Raised in that castle where the king was god
as a daughter, legitimacy almost irrelevant

4

I watched her spin straw to gold, thinking,

So this is what a Christian does—

>relentlessly preparing meals
>for hundreds of others over the years
>with little variety and no complaint—
>a simple menu to satisfy simple needs
>
>sewing bindings on discarded blankets
>to cover the grandchildren of an elderly neighbor
>whose daughter was killed and whose children's care
>had fallen to the aged survivor
>
>transforming our roach-ridden city apartment
>at Christmas-time with a hand-painted sheet
>of Mary and Jesus suspended in air
>over a city that could have been ours.

What choice did she have when it all began
but to trust that all her good work
her devotion to him and their open future
> would be enough
to buy the cranberries and popcorn needed
> to decorate the family tree?

CONDEMNED

Our house was not condemned
but the one behind us where Betty lived
was, and not only she but Mary and Lanny,
Rita and Donnie, their children, and Eunice
as well lived there, in six units, three on a side

overflowing with children so much so that
Eddie Wilson fell from a second-floor window.
Over the sill marking the fall
hung one of a pair of red drapes, the blood
on the ground below redder than the faded red
      of the drape above.

A yellow sign nailed to the wall of that house
read: This Building **CONDEMNED**.
Department of Public Health. I knew
what those heavy black capitals meant,
the stigma attached to anyone living there.

Nobody moved. The city did not evict.
But living under that interdict was the shame
of Hester Prynne. Shared shame, but nevertheless,
unlike the oblivious Pearl
the children involved knew they were powerless.

We moved from that house when I was twelve
thereby escaping a visible wound of black
and yellow on the front door,
like the Star of David worn by Jews
on their jackets in the Second World War.

6

On a visit to that neighborhood
I found buildings razed, gone—trees
and broken cement foundations
all that was left
of a war zone lost in time.

Ditching

of the smaller, younger
ones unable to defend themselves
against bigger, older
boys on bigger sleds

who forced the smaller
off the hill
into the ditch.

Not satisfied with
burying the face in snow
they forced that snow

down the back of the neck
their laughter at tears
the warm reward

for skilled maneuvering
of sled into sled.
Why else would they do such a thing
if not for the tears?

Kapishes' Back Yard

On entering Kapishes' back yard
I was Alice descending the rabbit hole
into a world unknown before goldfish
grew to the size of golden carp of Chinese tale
propelling their languorous, shimmering
bodies around the perimeter of a dug pond
under the apple trees in spring bloom.

O lost May.
O Kapish goldfish whose fate I know
not these 50 years hence, no doubt
you've gone the way of fish
the way of sparrow through mead hall
the way of all who swim, who fly
through this world with flourish of wing or fin

or hurry like Alice after the Rabbit
himself hurrying not to be late
for that very important date,
for that very important date.

The Men at Lincoln Square

wore overcoats
and could blow their noses
between their thumb and index finger
over the gutter neat as can be.
I tried it but it didn't work for me.

The lucky ones had cigarettes
a felt hat
a pint in the pocket.
They hung in hallways
like bats against the walls.

Sometimes they smiled at us children
as we made our way past them to matinees.
I wanted to take their winter hands
in mine and bring them inside the theater.
I wanted to spend my candy money on them.

I wanted to hear them laugh out loud
at cartoons, Martin and Lewis, newsreels
anything to bring them alive in the bright darkness
that for long moments
walled judgment outside.

Tony's Candy Store

*The importance of sweets in the life of a child
struggling against a bitter taste
can never be overestimated.*

Behind the store's fly-specked windows,
interior lit by a hanging bulb
Tony presided over circus peanuts
squirrel bars, bull's eyes, candy corn,
pastel-colored dots on strips of paper.

He rode the bus to Brookfield Street
summer and winter, climbed the hill
turned left on Milton, then right on Edgeworth
to his store where a nickel could raise a day
to Good & Plenty, Bonomo's Taffy,

Bit-O-Honey goes a long, long way.
Powdered Kool-Aid puckered lips
and colored tongues. A dime would buy
a Table Talk pie, one French horn
or two scoops of vanilla ice cream.

I nominate for sainthood such a man,
his miracles over the years outnumbering
three required for canonization, their form—
hope, for the child with pennies or nickel empalmed
asking for a bit of sweetness in the daily round.

Bobby

Periodically you would return
from wherever your parents sent you
for months at a time.
                      I remember you
on your bicycle, bent over handlebars,
cats' tails attached and blowing
straight back with the speed of wind
you created.
                    I stood in a wake
of fear as you passed, taking the corner
skidding in sand, building speed
to recover whatever the flying tails
gave you, Killer of Cats.
                    We all knew
having seen them hanging
from trees in your yard
two or three at a time, another kind
of strange fruit.
                    You flew by
a disturber of dreams with handlebar
pinwheel, cats' tails, high-pitched laugh
at the joke only you understood.

Katy

That you lived above a candy store
was blessing and compensation
when as a child you shared your hoard

with us, who after the first excitement
didn't notice the scar but focused
on candy instead.

The dog who bit you never knew
any shame you felt in your twisted smile
when you grew to be a teenaged girl

brown eyes doing all they could to compensate
for the unstrung bow of your mouth.
A cheerleader shouting as loud as the rest

half-smile beaming, elegant Katherine
cut to Katy— you cheered
for all of the meaning
of what was left.

I'll Show You, Freddie

I was four years old when my bete noire
had his violent way with me
because he could in our neighborhood.

My back yard was his front yard
an alley of dirt between our houses
where he held me down and beat me up.

Bigger is better is stronger is power
in fists and shoulders and weapons of war.
Too bad for the babies who got in the way

Of this black-haired dog of a soldier boy
who patrolled the supposed DMZ
of the no-man's land of our back yard.

His family moved. Was it then
I began to believe in God?
In miracles? In transformation of setting?

More likely I made the child's wish to be bigger
and stronger and smarter than he'd ever be.

Albie

He opened the gate in the picket fence
his black shock of hair a cock's comb.
At half his height and white as a hen
standing among summer flowers, his mother
who tended zinnias, roses, nasturtiums
tangling at her feet, kissed his cheek
and patted his back as Albie closed the gate,
and in jeans, t-shirt, and cigarette,
joined us kids at the corner to watch
the city workers clean the sewer
where North and Milton met at Witkin's Market.

The smell from that subterranean garden
drew us out of sleep and down the hill
for a summer ritual that wanted attending.
The mechanical arm on the back of the truck
was the stem of a metal flower whose petals
opened and dropped into the sewer
to gather whatever bouquets lay hidden
beneath black slime, dripping off slabs of wood
off a cat that might have been white once
bricks, stones, whatever was thrown into the gutter
up on the hill, and washed down in spring
run-offs that rushed no less than storied streams
in airy mountains out West somewhere do.

Jackie

Wearied of others' taunts
at 13, Jackie Strong
hanged himself

in the family's kitchen
above the store
that supplied the food

that fattened him
like a fall hog readied
for slaughter.

Taller than most
fatter than all
with bristling butch

and bright blue eyes,
cheeks as rosy
as his mother's florid complexion—

a woman three times
Jackie's size, in bedroom slippers,
anger and fear

in her red eyes
evident even to the child
of a visiting friend—

my mother,
who understood
the dynamic

recognized the man
who sat at the table drinking
from brown bottles

summer and winter
in an undershirt
that revealed his hairy torso.

Which taunt toppled
the wooden chair
that Sunday morning

while the others slept?
I heard them. I saw them
tossing the rope

over the transom
daring him
to go to a place

they didn't dare.
A scapegoat standing in?
They were fine with that.

Icon

Shirley Peterson burned in her yard
next door to mine when I was a child.

If I had known I could have watched
as I later watched Buddhist monks on TV
self-immolate to protest the Vietnam War.

I'd seen pictures of Joan of Arc.
Tied to a stake she couldn't outrun the fire,
different from Shirley burning

who ran from the moment
of striking the match.
Swathed in cotton, she was a torch.

A blazing candle
she burned and screamed and burned
until her mother snuffed her out

she was Cinderella,
borne mournfully off in a wailing coach
her skin curling about her
in smoking tatters.

Charred star of the neighborhood
she returned home months later
with grace that hadn't possessed her before
pain crowned her limbs and carriage.

A quiet queen, she would sit on the steps
of her back porch, watching the play,

holding the handrail lightly
her bandaged arm cushioning her hidden face.

Mrs. Jaatinen

The dull clink of the wooden cane
on the water pipes summoned my mother
as did the mournful *Esteri!* we could hear
through the floor in the back of the house
when Mrs. Jaatinen needed to use the chair,
needed my mother to be the half
of her body rendered useless by stroke.

I followed my mother downstairs
hoping to sample from Whitman's boxes
stacked three high on the oak bureau,
gifts from friends who themselves enjoyed
a friendly rummage among soft and hard
centers, when they sat for a visit in wheelchair,
on bed's end or standing by the window—

Gusti Hill, his low chuckle,
humped back and felt hat

Mary Ramsey with pasty face
netted hair and black eyes

Massive Mrs. Kyllonen smelling
of something unidentified

all chattered to Mrs. in Finn
and she to them, gesturing

with her right hand, her left
a helpless mitten in her lap.

I wonder now why they never moved
her iron bed beneath the window
where at least at night she could have
looked up and seen a handful of stars.

Dependence

The dependence of plants reminds me of women.
Suppose they're housed with a crazy man
who talks about pouring boiling water
       into their pots.
Their foliage trembles in panic
stands up on the backs of their stems.

Why don't they leave the brute, you say.
Get up and go. They can't, I say.
It's not that easy; they're rooted.

Downstairs Neighbor

Mrs. Waters opened her door
at the end of an unlighted corridor. Half
her face visible, she asked,
What do you want?
I'm collecting money for the school playground
I answered, in the trembling tone
of a seven-year-old. She turned from me

to fetch her purse, and the door swung open
like a storyteller. I peered in, seeking
signs of the pet rat our neighbor
reported she kept and fed pieces of cheese.
No rat, but a Coca Cola freezer, piles of newspapers
two Table Talk pie tins filled with beans
all hallowed in the candlepower
of a single lightbulb dangling over the table.

I felt I looked into an animal's lair
drawn and repulsed at the same time
filled with silent wonder before
this seeing how it was for her
whose hand reached out a dime, a nickel
her part in the redemption of slide, of swings,
of sandbox and seesaw for schoolyard
       and neighborhood play.

On Hearing Finnish Spoken after Many Years

Whispered words in Finnish conjure
talk between two women I knew as a child

exchanging news
at a table covered with oilcloth
their words covered with hidden meaning.
Between them they knew what they meant.

I needed to be content with nissu*
and coffee laced with sugar and milk
while what I really wanted
      to take and eat
      to take and drink

was their love for each other
hidden in language
I couldn't understand.

*Finnish sweet bread

Saturday Sauna

In the steamy dark of the evening sauna
surrounded by voices of sisters, cousins, of aunts
who are mothers, including my own

young eyes grow accustomed
to pale bodies, young ears to the pitch
and hiss of water on stones

hot stones, heaving out breath
to the heights of wooden tiers where we sit,
washing in our history with yellow soap.

Conjuring My Mother

I'll use anything for conjuring—
an old baked bean recipe
written in my mother's hand
wishing that I somehow could
be the very paper on which she'd writ molasses.

Reclaiming

delicate scissors left on a shelf
by a man who died in the basement apartment
of the house I lived in as a child

whose legend had buried him under the floor
of the room one entered terrified
out of unelectrified darkness into half light.

Over the secret earth we hurried
my sister and I, to the next room.
Thieves both we took the scissors

terror shaking my knees and constricting my throat.
I can't breathe Barbara.
Let's leave before he comes and kills us.

She flew for the stairs with me behind
and behind me the threat of him
holding silver threads he needed cut.

Up the second flight we panted, calling *Mom!*
who was there, opening the door to our apartment.
We hid between her apron and her skirt.

Barbara said, *Look what we found*
in Ira's house. A pair of scissors.
My mother, a seamstress, liked them immediately.

My Mother Hanging Clothes in January

I remember her
knuckles swollen red
through zero hours
of long johns icing on the line.

Wind in the ropes
of the tiered reel
wrung the sheets
from her grappling hand
and practically pulled her
over the railing
into the dead space
between three-deckers
where nothing ever survived.

Through hangings and dryings
safe I prayed her
with marvelous faith
in my own small power to pray
while under the hurrying shadows of houses
she'd unbend and peel frozen clothes
from lines
laughing as she walked the johns
into the darkening room
where children were.

Bringing Up the Oil

The range oil we burned
came from ports we couldn't imagine
to our tiny cavity of cold in the side of a hill

pumped into barrels that rested like ships
in steel cradles on a sea floor, derelict hulks
from wars past or submarines hidden beneath
      the building's surface.

Deep-sea divers, my sister and I
descended nightly to unlighted depths
where we learned to see in the dark

huddling together against the cold
to unlock the barrel, the pain of icy metal on flesh
acute. If the key wouldn't turn for shiv'ring

we held firm and jiggled the spigot
to tumble the lock. The kerosene flowed.
We screwed on the spring cap, locked the barrel

and began the climb, each of us holding
half the handle, balancing the pressure
on our cupped hands.

By synchronizing our child steps
and resting every third stair
we had no bends, ascending back
      up into the light.

Runaways

At the altar of Our Lady of the Angels
Church I prayed for myself and a friend
for safety. We were nine and running away
from certain punishment, possible jail-time.
We thought the vandalism we had done

enough to put us away for years.
We'd heard about the Reformatory
from boys in our neighborhood and knew
there was something like that for girls.
We could be the first to test its limits.

Ten miles we walked in deepening dusk.
No city streetlight shone, where we turned left
in that country place and came to the house
of a friend who'd moved from our neighbor-
hood the year before.

The shock on her mother's face at seeing
us at her back door marked the beginning
of our travail. What stayed with me
over the years was not the anger, not the punishment,
but the guidance we received in that deepening dusk.

Ironing and Smoking

My fingers don't have the elegant length
of yours with the pinkie bent in the middle
at rest, but still in the thousand wrinkles
early in my hands, your thin skin shines

as did burns from the iron on the heel
of your hand, the wrist, the flesh of the forearm
distracted as you were by television
squinting through cigarette smoke to see

Don Ameche romancing on Channel 4
returning you for those few hours
to movie theaters where Myrna Loy
stood in for you with Clark Gable.

(You filled a shoebox with your pencil portraits of him.)

No wonder you married him after three weeks.
Movie-star handsome, people said of your husband
Clark Gable by day, with a dash of Durante for humor
but Lon Chaney at night.

I watched you simmer at the ironing board
turning your wedding band 'round and 'round
turning the smoke carefully over
silently in your mouth before you exhaled.

The Morning after Payday

How much money is left? she asked.
I rummaged through my father's pockets,
the wallet empty, but two dollars
and ten cents in the pants.

Two dollars and ten cents
dropped like a curtain through morning light
and spread a pall of dread like oil
over the kitchen table.

With milk at fifty cents a gallon,
thank goodness someone had given us
powdered, its chalky lumps
the calcium we needed to grow

and show that children do survive
dire circumstances, their will
to live a hidden badge, shiny from
resisting all they must oppose.

Spelling Czechoslovakia

Spelling Czechoslovakia
in bed at night to my brother and sister,
the joy of C-Z-E-C-H- etcetera
was knowing
there was another place
on the other side of the sea.

I climbed aboard that spelling bark
each night and sailed through waves
of words that parted as I spelled my way
across boundaries of my known world
toward a country
I never could have predicted.

Sacred Ground

I found the bird
in our grassless yard where the glass grew.
Had it hoped for a worm in that dry place?
Did it fall unlucky from the sky?

Like Tobit stealthily burying the dead
thrown outside the walls of Ninevah, I
put the bird in a pasteboard box
and carrying my book of *Prayers for the Dead*
walked up the hill, a funeral procession of one

into the field and past the mattress
where sometimes a drunk was sleeping off
his Friday night on Saturday morning,
to the oak where I'd buried a host of others—
snake skins, insects, anything dead.

I dug the grave under the oak
with a hardy spoon from my mother's kitchen
then laid the box into the ground
to rot around the bird who too would rot
wrapped in its shroud of toilet paper

while I vested in shorts and top
asked the God of the living and dead
to raise this bird to new life
through Christ. Amen

Miss Cronin's Room

Students bussed from around the city
were all in place by 8 o'clock
when she turned the key to lock her door. *Click*.
Only a fire drill, death in a family, the final bell

could turn that key
in the days before Special Ed had a name.
Miss Cronin's red lipstick, her Joan-
of-Arc pageboy of black hair
her sheer size and black eyes

could shrivel skin with nary a word
and protect her charges from scapegoating.
On recess duty her circle of power
surrounded them like a force of nature
and heaven. Once I carried a message

from another teacher to her fort. I shrank
into my knocking hand as I heard the key turn,
her friendly smile
when she opened the door
a shock to my child system.

Jounces

Along a city brook with its naked banks
teenaged boys in dungarees swung
on ropes strung high from trees all dead
of creeping Dutch elm disease.
I clung to my mother's skirt
as we passed them by
maneuvering between parked cars
baby leading the crying way
in the carriage across tar and grass
to the playground where we pumped above
that neighborhood on swings that meant
flying high in chains above the bar.

The Friday Night Fights

> *To look sharp and to feel sharp too*
> *Use a razor that is made for you:*
> *Light, regular, heavy—*
> *For the quickest, slickest shave of all.*

Sponsored by Gillette, the Friday night fights
found my father in his favorite chair, ale
at the ready, calling to me in the kitchen,
Make me a sandwich. Bologna with butter
    and mustard on pumpernickel!

I joined him in front of the television
to witness his joy as two men
pummeled each other. He'd rise from his seat
as the tension rose—4...5...6—the referee counted
toward 10, but the boxer was on his feet again

not unlike my father, who had fallen,
and fallen, but always managed to rise again
to see if his feet could still dance
around the confining ring of his life
taking punch after punch, bloodied, but look

he's up again, refusing the call
of a TKO, wanting a clear
knockout. It's what he got at the last,
bologna sandwich half eaten, he couldn't
get up off the canvas, couldn't get up
        to answer the final bell.

After Seamus Heaney's "Seeing Things III"

Heaney's vision of his drowned father
coming toward him in the yard
recalls to me my own father
whom I did not know,
except as an innocent child
knows the joy of the swim
at day's end—that's how I knew him

unashamed of his pale, aging frame
his teeth a-chatter
as he strode in the water
lifting his arms like the wings of an angel
he was to me, all of that
and a teller of tales, fall-down-laughing tales
of him as a boy.

And trying to imagine
his thick fingers as young talons
clutching
the back of the newspaper truck at dawn
in his neighborhood.
                      A free ride,
that's all he ever sought or wanted.

He invited us all along
and we tried to cling to that truck with him
in summer, to hook our sleds in winter
but we ditched in snowbanks along the road
and could not follow him toward the sun
rising in the distance he was hurrying toward.

Aiden Kieli*

I'm about the business of learning Finnish
tricking out my mother's life by tens
of letters in single words: k's, n's, omnipresent
o's struggle with my western speech for dominance.

I fall back to lullaby, then
meet with resistance at the early hour
of Anglicization, acculturation
in a neighborhood where a different majority ruled.

In my majority I choose her language
and feel the gates of the sluiceway lift
when I dive down
in a rush of syllables, trusting when I surface

again, I'll surface in Finland,
my keel, my rudder,
my compass—my mother tongue.

*Finnish for mother tongue

Mourning Anew

Mourning anew for my father
you say neatly, It was a life.

The ceiling opens to cherubim,
trumpets flare, champagne bottles
uncork.
               Uncorked himself
at 46 his life flowed out in moments.
Who-is became what-was

all promise and reform
of the old life into the new.
Just as it was, you say,

just those years with everything
they contained—
it was a life

to be honored as such
not wishing it more or different.
It was what it was.

You're better for it.
Dismiss the sentinels of regret.
They've earned their sleep

as has he. Let him go on
in his death—his life, now.

Poets Hill
    for Liz Bailey

Years have passed
since we met at a party
and reminisced about Worcester, Mass.

where you grew up on Poets Hill,
on Hemans Street in the North End
named for the nineteenth-

century poet, you explained. Your street
completed the neighborhood bounded
by Milton, Dryden, Byron—

                      the information
a shock, for I too had spent my childhood
there, but on Milton Street, never thinking

of those famous names as anything other
than reference points for candy stores
or friends' houses. I went in search of

the marker you noted, designating
Poets Hill, on the Common where
we both had played on swings,

had climbed up the down slide
had drunk from the spring at the edge
of the field, now occupied by legions

of homes, the once greensward now
a faded invitation underfoot, unopened,

unread through seasons of years since

we lived there. No matter. The Hill
lives on in me, and in you who walk
in the offing, arm-in-arm with Byron

whose life was lost early, whose name
is that of the marginal street,
the limit of Poets Hill—the North End.

Q. Why Don't You Move South for the Winter?

It's as simple as rosy fingers of dawn
at quarter of seven
reaching into God's line of vision

as simple as crow pecking at bones
on the compost heap
covered with snow

as simple as branch of stag sumac
rimed in frost
already anticipating night's cold

when we will sit by candlelight
watching the fire
refusing the flip of a switch.

Porpentine

Make each particular hair to stand an end,
Like quills up on the fretful porpentine.
                        Hamlet Act I, scene v.

I cohabitate with a porcupine
during the winter when he is dormant
only somewhat though, as his pile of pellets
tells. Understand, he's on the ground floor
while I am above in the writing house
courting a muse I increasingly think
moves slowly in a body covered with quills.

Metaphysician in Overshoes

Thoreau walked in overshoes
across the tundra of Walden Pond
fish wondering at the winter fool
as they sleepily watched his shadowy foot
pass over, truant from another school
treading ideas as they did water
in the open stillness of life alone.

March to Spring

Smoke from my writing house chimney
overtakes me as I walk in the woods,
dipping down before the rain, friendly
like an animal—a cat perhaps, or even
a sinuous snake.

              It filters through braided limbs
of hemlock and leads me into the deeper
wood, where the white flag of winter's
surrender retreats, the freed ground telling
its victory with a thousand green tongues.

Secular Sainthood

I toast Ben Franklin with tea
as I toast beside the Jotul stove,
successor to the eponymous
Franklin, which adorns still many
a parlor in Maine, and enables long
and warm dreams of another time
when chilblains ruled, and a prophet/
inventor arose to democratize heat.

The Ides of March

I would have thought it another Wednesday, ordinary
in its round of appointments, including hours
set aside to free the poem caught between
morning vapors and evening mists lifting
    off the meadow.

But ordinary turns out to be the furthest from
what turns at center today, a weariness at news
of death—more death in Iraq, on the obits page,
three students from URI drowned, bodies found today.
In Hawaii a levee collapsed, number of dead
not yet counted, and now I read Heaney's tribute
to Hugh, shot dead, in Northern Ireland

        years ago
        but present here on the Ides of March
        in Heaney's poem "Keeping Going"
        on this my own dead father's birthday,
        come 'round again with wild weather—
        turbulent squalls of snow succeeded
        by sun, recalling last night's lunar eclipse
        the moon startling bright
        as it fully emerged from earth's penumbra
        sure as a shaft of shadow cast
        like a glance of God down my Jobian soul.

Fragment

Fittingly
"Fragment" is the first whole poem
    (on p. 23 of *Pictures from Brueghel*
        and other poems by William Carlos Williams)
that remains intact.

I found the remains this morning
in a pine grove out back, half-hidden
by needles and winter leaves.

Was it mice chewed
the torn white pages
unglued and wedded to earth by snow—

black words on white paper
imprinted and numbered page by page
the cover spattered and torn

in pieces, leavings of insects and God-knows-
what-else lay or burrowed into this text,
looking for protection Williams

didn't factor in. In "Fragment"
he writes

as for him who
finds fault
may silliness

and sorrow
overtake him
when you wrote

you did not
know
the power of
your words

Did he understand the power
of his own to attract—

to be carried somehow from my writing house
to this grove by unseen
hand—or claw on paw
of a heaving creature
longing for what it couldn't name?
But Williams could
in the section and other poems,
growing lichen and pressed together
in a damp community of words.

I decided the creature was larger than mouse—
the arc of its bite, three quarters of an inch
with a delicate edge as of pinking shears
small shears to be found in a house
built by a writer of children's books
and piercing pp. 23 through 45,

47 reduced to one toothmark
just on the edge, making it less than perfect.

But who can speak of perfection now?
Spots of mold purplish to gray
like those on the forehead of late middle age
mottle the upper half of 47.

Only the start of part III, To all the girls
of all ages
who walk up and down on

the streets of this town
silent or gabbing
putting—

only this is without blemish.
"*Perpetuum Mobile*," Williams called it
and well he might have
his living text resurrected from soil

no less than Christ, giving life
(*perpetuum mobile*) not only to girls
but to the whale above in "Histology,"
to the sumac in "Exercise..." that died,
as well as to the unnamed creature
who hauled it away.

And I? I found the text
missing since fall.
I've brought it into my house
to translate the signs.

Listen, Look

Through the window, through branches
of pine, over the lawn to lilac in bloom
beyond, it's raining. The tin roof a-rattle,
I remove spectacles to allow a blur
of sight and sound. Nothing clear may
open a way for everything clear in a new
way of seeing meaning as green as it is
this early May morning in Maine.

Graduation Day, Eastport, Maine

In the derelict boatyard of the boat building school
We walk among wrecks on a cloudy day
Noting the marks of student work
—holes plugged, paint scraped—
A sigh of eternal patience breathes at center.

Here I think of my living will,
My body promised to a medical school
Whose students, like these rebuilders of boats
Will bend to the task of a derelict hulk
To learn how to make one better and keep it afloat.

First Cigarette

> "our poems can never satisfy us,
> since they are at best a diminished echo
> of a song that maybe once or twice
> in a lifetime we've heard
> and keep trying to recall"
> Stanley Kunitz in "Reflections," from
> *The Collected Poems*

as I recall you told me about
your first cigarette that summer working
at Goudy & Stevens shipyard in Boothbay, Maine.

All blood and muscle at nineteen
a stripling assigned to oil the teak
hull of a customer's ketch

you rowed to the mooring with Bob
dropped your Pepsi over the side
into the frigid Maine water

to cool until your break at 12 o'clock.
Rubbing through the June morning
sun on your back, all was caress.

At noon you pulled your Pepsi line.
A glassy-eyed fish
it broke the surface. You offered Bob

a swig, and he in turn proffered you
a cigarette, a Lucky Strike.
Why not? you thought, and stuck

the unfamiliar between your lips
inhaling as though
you'd been doing it

all your life—the lightheaded high
not qualified by watery eye
or cough, when the nicotine

dappled your lung and blood
as the sun dappled the water.
For a dozen years you sought that first

satisfaction of linseed-oiled
rag on teak, sun on water
cigarette smoke deep in the learning lung.

Cutting My Daughter's Hair Down by the Pasture

We chat of inconsequential things—
Ginger's calf overdue
a week, is it? she asks
her blue eyes questioning me.

Four days, I think since the moon was full
and we all expected that to draw it out
I answer, distracted
charmed by the red in her hair
that draws a cloud of dead grandmothers
to roil and hover aloft over what we do.

Watching for the Haymaker

Have you forgotten the fields edged with daisies
and black-eyed Susans beginning to dot here and
there the daisies' eyes? Do you know the timothy
is headed up, ready, wanting to be cut down?

All are on tiptoe, these fields of grass, looking
for you down the road, listening for the clank
and groan of the tractors hauling the mower,
the baler and you, with your John Deere cap
askew, off to the left, a green and welcome sight.

I forgot to tell you...

There were ducks at dusk on the Kennebec
River, while you were inside buying ice cream.
I thought they were stones at first
eight of them piled near the shore

the smaller stones suddenly moving
and assuming the shape of ducks
discernible in the shifting light
that enabled seeing in a new way.

They ducked and paddled in close
arcs among the grasses
before turning their heads
to the softness of their feathered beds.

Cheers!

'Though I stand in the fields of green summer
the Puritan landscape of winter lurks in my mind
like a stern mother, arms crossed over her breast
reminding me this will not last.

The porridge will harden, the shadows lengthen.
No substance, no habit will keep at bay
the descent of absolute winter on the waiting world.

Day of Darkness

On the nineteenth of May in 1780 a day of darkness
alarmed creation, acclaimed as you might expect
    The Day of Judgment

known in the roosting of fowl
peeping of frog
the noisy night bird calling at noon.

Candles were lit and stoics
ate their beef and bread pudding,
then wiped their mouths in a tidy way

while outside others wrung their hands
crying, This is the end!
The day of reckoning!

They fell on their knees
in the dirt and begged for mercy.
But mercy proved unnecessary

when scientific minds of the time
noticed the scum on water collected
in barrels and keeping pools.

On closer inspection the residue
of burnt leaves was identified, and news
passed of fires in northern New England

glad to send its sulphur and brimstone
South, where long-faced Bay Staters
numbered their sins and crying, tried to atone.

Be-fogged in Maine: A Visitation

A lobster boat appeared in the fog
where consternated, you in the cockpit
of your own boat, drifting, unsure
which way to steer—not to the thorny
ledges—but to Pemaquid and from there
to Boothbay and home.

            The lobsterman's voice
was clear and calm in the shifting fog,
his yellow sou'wester the only shape
that could be detected.

            Follow my buoys, he said.
He held one up for you to see its colors.
You throttled up and followed the line
to the bell buoy and thence to Pemaquid
where fog lifted, relief settled, and
in the distance Seguin marked the horizon.

For Philip Booth, Still

You wrote of rock and sea
in Maine, where you grew to be
like them, all hairy with lichen
and wave-tossed in older age;
like the hemlocks that still stand
on tidal ledges, you yourself
stood sentinel, witness to Arcturus,
to Venus, Polaris, who finally
guided you off the ledges, thence
across the water and on to home.

Rhubarb Lust

Other people's rhubarb
has leaves the size of the fans you see
in pictures in nineteenth-century books
of ancient Egypt or Babylon

the ones with stems to match, thick
as thumbs of sumo wrestlers, or of men
who might play professional ball.

Mind you, this rhubarb can grow
on the edge of other people's gardens
like a second cousin invited to dinner
only on special occasions

while I grateful for gifts of shoots
have coddled them into the ground
by the humus pile on the down slope
or heeled them into the fertile crescent

of our vegetable garden, where life
burgeons—turnips with nary a scab
tomatoes to make an Italian
       grandmother weep—

but rhubarb in that vegetable Eden?
Spinster stalks with stingy leaves
and deeper into their pale green
stinginess, multiple holes.

What can that be but rhubarb kharma?
Did I fail to tend a plot somewhere

in the past? Was I one who took a patch
for granted, left it to bolt and wither
         for want of care?

I cast wide into metaphysics
having exhausted explanations
in the natural realm
where I cultivate rhubarb lust.

Early on a Late August Morning

Dropping
handkerchiefs in the grass

Hanging
chandeliers in the bushes

Cinderella spiders are having a ball.

When first I lit the October stove

When first I lit the October stove
a grasshopper planted his sticky
feet on a pane of glass in one
of the house's windows.

I tapped the pane with my finger-
nail; he moved a leg in response.
Whether conversation or nervous
reaction, communication was

established, 'though I suspect it
was warmth from the stove held
his cold-bloodied belly there,
pressed to the glass, readying

himself for a day of carousing
to scandalize the industrious ant,
and give joy to us who
admire his high-jumping ways.

Open Season

A hen turkey hurries across the field
like a big-bosomed woman hugging
her purse and hurrying after a departing

bus. But this turkey has an extra incentive
beyond the chicks who wait at home,
her very life is on the line in this open
season on turkeys that starts today.

In morte vita

The marriage next door has crumbled.
He has gone and gotten a haircut,
his first professional cut in 20 years.

No longer the wife wielding scissors
she has set the dangerous instruments down
and cut a path through the woods with the edge of her mind.

Through the classifieds in a magazine
he's selling chains and pickup parts
odd things he won't be needing anymore.

And she has given her art away
created from crumbs dropped from the table.
She says she's ready now to consume the loaf.

Relationship

His friend sent a satellite view of my son's house to him
by e-mail, through cyberspace,
the picture said all about how that friend
was thinking of him and where he was

his roof nestled among other roofs
in a neighborhood of city trees
that name the streets they grow from
      —Oak, Maple, Elm—
and house birds in canopies

that rustle and fret outside my son's window.
And now this morning at my writing house
full frontally flaring like twin escutcheons
two chickadees peck at the window, then

fly up and away back to the house
where I follow and find their empty dish
fill it again as they filled me
with more than seed by knowing where I was.

Trying to Take Responsibility

The year of resolve I put on boots
and join him in the chicken-killing yard.
Why should he be alone in managing death?
He cuts off a chicken's head,
ropes her by her feet to the hay elevator
to let her drain. Whack!

He strings the second one up.
Blood thickly drips. Water boils
on the Coleman stove. He dunks the first
to loosen the feathers.
Unspeaking he hands the hen to me.

I hold her by her horny feet, pulling
at masses of white feathers
bloodied now. The soundless tears
begin, and what is left of fowl jerks in my hand.

Train in Gardiner

Josh, I watch this train for you
and for myself, I hear the whistle blow
advancing along the Kennebec
railboxthenationalboxcarpool
bangorandaroostookhookerchemicalsconrail
pass
mainecentralthepinetreeroutecaboose
to Boston, and Maine left behind
in reaches of Kennebec and Sheepscot rivers
where tides turn and salmon spawn
you're gone, the way of trains.

About the Author

Judith Robbins is the mother of four and a graduate of Bates College and Harvard Divinity School. She grew up on Milton Street in the North End of Worcester, Massachusetts, in an area called Poets Hill, the neighborhood she celebrates in this, her first collection. She moved to Maine in 1967 with her husband Jon, where she still lives and writes. Her first poem was published when she was seven, and she has since been widely published in magazines and journals, including *The Worcester Review,* *Puckerbrush Review,* and *The American Scholar.*

www.ingramcontent.com/pod-product-compliance
Lightning Source LLC
LaVergne TN
LVHW011429080426
835512LV00005B/353